MW00439221

"I hated prog rock. No soul. Adrian thinks CX has been high jacked by a similar wasted effort. I'd agree we need to connect more than conceive as far as customer experience is concerned. Or miss the point entirely. Punk CX does the job of jarring us back to our senses."
Martin Hill-Wilson - *Deadhead CX Strategist*

"Be courageous. Be political. Be you. In Punk CX, Adrian Swinscoe makes the point superbly, marrying form and function effing well."
Minter Dial, *speaker, award-winning filmmaker and author of Futureproof and Heartificial Empathy*

At SimplyBusiness we've never been scared to go our our own way and it's worked for us. In Reboot, I advocated for a different type of business given the challenges that we now face in our society. With Punk CX, Adrian turns up the volume and has produced not only a manifesto for real change but also a manual that will help you really stand out amongst your peers.....only if you are brave enough to step up.
Jason Stockwood, *Vice Chair - Simply Business*

If you're looking for the usual style of business book, this is not it! Honestly, that's a good thing. There are times when people need something pithier and perhaps a little more in-your-face to make them stand up and take notice. This book is just that. Adrian asks the tough questions in a no-bullshit kind of way that slaps you upside the head and begs the question, "Seriously, what are you really doing about the customer experience?"
Annette Franz, *Founder and CEO of CX Journey Inc*

"One look at this book and you know you're in for an experience. It's stylish, important, convenient, brave, funny, loud and fun. Not what you would expect from a business book about customer experience! Loved it!"
Shep Hyken, *customer service/experience expert and New York Times bestselling author*

"Adrian Swinscoe delivers with Punk CX. He strips down customer experience to its essence. Just as punk music was about keeping it honest, this book will force you to rethink how you view your customer's experience. It is a bold statement, a call to action, and a must read."
Stan Phelps, *Founder of PurpleGoldfish.com, Author of the Goldfish Series*

In Punk CX, Adrian Swinscoe eschews fussy frameworks and meticulous metrics in favour of a back-to-basics approach that will appeal to all readers, regardless of whether they are already managing a customer experience programme or starting out in the world of CX. This is Swinscoe's manifesto to prevent customer experience management from disappearing up its own backside. So never mind the bollocks, read Punk CX for a short, sharp, shot of customer experience advice.
Neil Davey, *Managing Editor, MyCustomer.com*

"In his new book, Adrian Swinscoe takes a deeply humanistic and thoughtfully critical look at the discipline of Customer Experience. His writing urges us to think of customers as people first and only then consider technology, methodology, process, and all the trendy and increasingly meaningless CX and UX jargon and clichés. Adrian's latest work is f'ing brilliant and I am jealous that I did not come up with such a novel idea and fun and engaging execution. I will be re-reading it for some time to come."
Alexander Genov, *Head of Customer Research, Zappos*

"Practical tips, inspiring insights and interviews with a simple message: Humans First. Make sure people know they matter. Cx=Ex"
Carrie Duarte, *Workforce of the Future Leader at PwC*

"A beautifully designed book, full of fresh and provocative ideas to challenge your thinking"
Richard Shotton, *Head of Behavioural Science at MG OMD and author of The Choice Factory.*

"Customer centricity is a mentality, not a metric, and Punk CX nails it."
Nick Francis, *Co-founder & CEO at Help Scout*

ADRIAN came up with the words and ideas
TOM & MATT coloured things in
OISIN checked the spelling

~~MGMT~~
~~L'SHIP~~
PUNK CX
~~BIZ~~

ISBN: 9781095272015

Design concept by Adrian Swinscoe, Tom Watts & Matt Wilson
Front cover and book design by Tom Watts & Matt Wilson
Editing by Oisin Lunny

Note: The sources for all unattributed data references are available on request.

Printed by relentless.com

First printing edition 2019.

Punk CX
91 Lansdowne Place
Hove, East Sussex BN3 1FN
U.K.
Tel: +44 (0)20 3239 2402
Email: books@adrianswinscoe.com
www.adrianswinscoe.com
www.punkcx.com

Big waves, huge thanks and loads of love to:

H
M&D also known as D&A
J
J, E, L, I and M
H's M
J,M & K
O,J & P'script
J&C
E
M,M,I & A
O
R
T&M

Prog rock as a ... emerged in the late 1960s and 1970s in the UK and the USA. Whilst popular it was often accused of being overly technical, over-produced, too elaborate, too complicated, inwardly focused, and a little aloof. The audience were often observers rather than participants and the genre was often in danger of disappearing up its own a***.

I think that the customer service and customer experience (CX) space is starting to exhibit some of the same characteristics as prog rock... namely it's becoming overly technical, benchmarked, frame-worked, measured, codified, certified, specialised and functionalised.

In fact, CX could also be accused of being in danger of disappearing up its own a*** too.

And, given the many reports that suggest that around 70% of customer experience projects fail to deliver on their promises, there is a danger that it is also losing sight of its real audience: the customer.

However, if we go back to the musical genre analogy, what happened next is the really interesting bit. Punk exploded out of the back of prog rock with its DIY ethic. It was inclusive, democratising, back to basics, punchy and brave. The approach was all heart, and the energy of Punk inspired both a cultural and

It dared to be different. And it was OK with the fact that not everyone liked that.

So, that got me to thinking.

What would a punk rock version of CX look and feel like?

This is what this book is about.

But, in keeping with a punk ethos it will not be traditional book.

It will not contain 50,000 words and another framework aimed at solving all of your problems.

A punk wouldn't do that.

A punk would just tell you what they thought, and then you would have to make up your own mind as to whether you liked it or not.

Therefore, the book will be short, to the point, full of ideas, possibly a bit shouty and profane in places (sorry Mum), and heavy on design.

Many folks may not like it.

And, that's ok :)

It is designed to inspire, annoy, make people think, and encourage them to be braver in their thinking and doing.

> **PUNK ROCK WAS A "BACK TO BASICS" MOVEMENT THAT OCCURRED IN THE MID-1970'S, IN REACTION TO THE INCREASING COMMERCIALISM AND AGEING OF THE PREVIOUS GENERATION OF ROCK STARS. MOST PUNK SONGS WERE SIMPLE TO PLAY, AS A REACTION TO THE INCREASING COMPLEXITY OF THE MUSIC OF PROGRESSIVE ROCK.**

The New York Times Guide to Essential Knowledge

PUNK IS...

AN ATTITUDE AND A MINDSET,

NOT A METHOD.

Not scared to do things differently
& flip things on their heads.

NOT THE ANSWER.

That is up to you.

"Punk is: the personal expression of uniqueness that comes from the experiences of growing up in touch with our human ability to reason and ask questions; a movement that serves to refute social attitudes that have been perpetuated through wilful ignorance of human nature; a process of questioning and commitment to understanding that results in self-progress, and through repetition, flowers into social evolution; a belief that this world is what we make of it, truth comes from our understanding of the way things are, not from the blind adherence to prescriptions about the way things should be; the constant struggle against fear of social repercussions."

Greg Graffin, co-founder of one of my favourite punk bands, Bad Religion.

"FORGIVE ME FOR WRITING A LONG LETTER AS I DID NOT HAVE TIME TO WRITE A SHORT ONE"

Blaise Pascal, the French mathematician, physicist and philosopher that lived in the 17th century and who was a noted letter writer.

In keeping with the music and punk theme, we have a track listing rather than a table of contents.

This book is like an album.

You might like it in its entirety but, equally, you might only like a few tracks.

It's up to you.

Here's a list of tracks:

THE WAY WE ARE

FOR PUNKS EVERYWHERE

FANS, FANS, FANS

DEMOS & B-SIDES

DIY

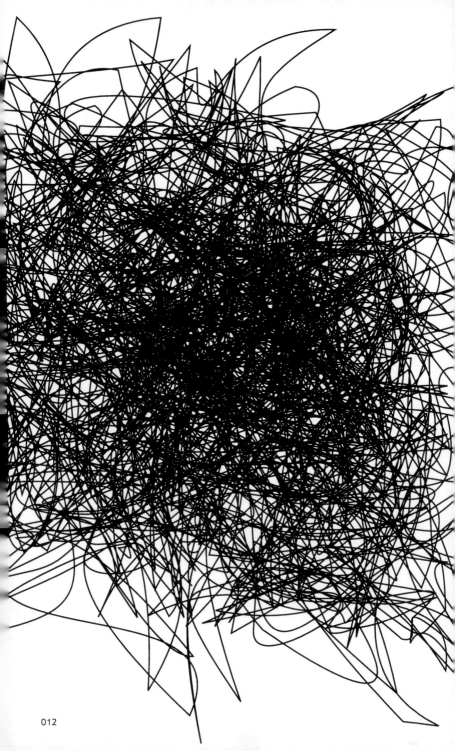

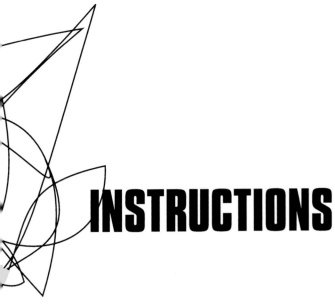

INSTRUCTIONS

Feel free to destroy this book.

Ignore/rip out/scrub out/graffiti on the tracks that
are not relevant to you and your organisation.

Alternatively, take a picture of them and send them
to someone who will find them relevant.

When you are done deciding out which tracks matter to you
and your organisation, get together with your team and figure
out what you are going to do about them.

ARE YOU AN ARTIST?

OR, ARE YOU JUST

COLOURING IN?

Too many customer experience programmes are formulaic affairs that produce expected yet disappointing results.

This is just like painting by numbers, you may create nice pictures but... it won't be art, and it definitely won't give you a chance of creating a masterpiece.

To really change this, we have to start with ourselves.

Do you want to be an artist, or someone that is good at colouring in?

When you have your answer, decide what you are going to do next?

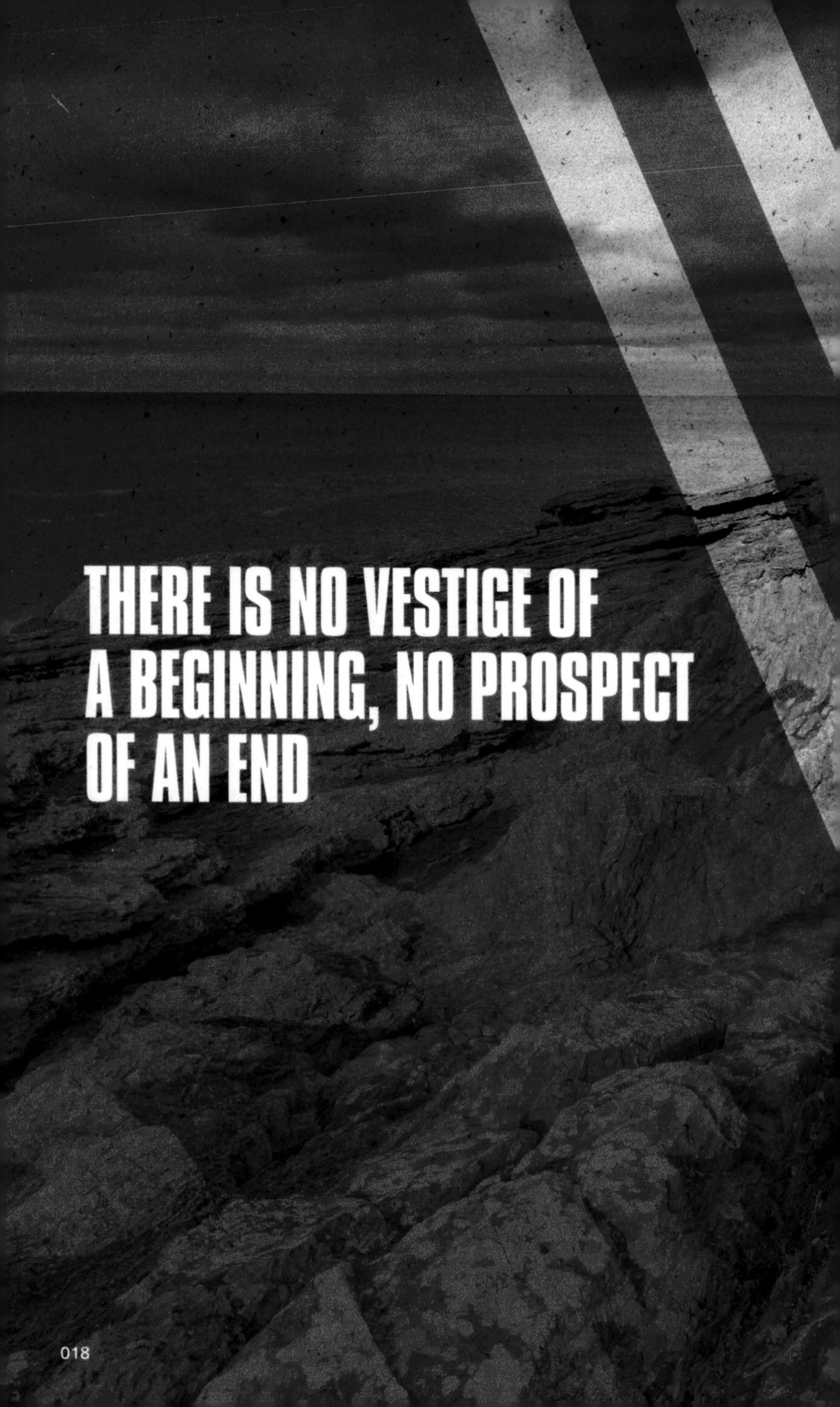

THERE IS NO VESTIGE OF
A BEGINNING, NO PROSPECT
OF AN END

I discovered this quote embedded in the song "No Control" by Bad Religion, a US punk band known for their tuneful songs and cerebral lyrics.

"There is no vestige of a beginning, no prospect of an end."

The actual quote comes from James Hutton's 1788 book *Theory Of The Earth*, which is acknowledged as one of the first treatises on geology.

The quote makes me think about all the transformation talk that continuously swirls around the industry. Transformation this, transformation that, transformation other.

Forgive me but can we STOP talking about digital and customer experience transformation? Or any other sort of transformation for

that matter.

Most transformation programs fail anyway.

Should we not be talking about *evolution* instead?

As James Hutton found in the 18th Century, things don't transform they just evolve with time, and there is "no vestige of a beginning, no prospect of an end".

So, the next time you start to think about yet another transformation project, just stop and ask yourself a few questions:

Do you *really* need to transform your business?

What problem is the 'transformation' project trying to solve?

Also, what is the emotional impact of a(nother) transformation project on your people?

If you just concentrated on evolving your business and people in line with what your customers need and want, what would happen?

YES, IT'S F—CKING POLITICAL

Brands have often shied away from political issues, not wanting to offend or alienate some of its customers.

However, according to Accenture's *14th Annual Global Consumer Pulse Research,* 62% of consumers worldwide want companies to take a stand on the social, cultural, environmental and political issues they care about.

In line with this we are increasingly seeing examples of brands that are becoming more and more political in their marketing campaigns, commentary and actions. And, they are being rewarded for it by their customers.

Nike chose Colin Kaepernick, a American quarterback who knelt during the national anthem to protest against police racism, as the face of one of its marketing campaigns in 2018.

Many people didn't like it but even more did. Their online sales rose 32% in the aftermath of the Kaepernick campaign, over 6% above the average industry growth rate.

Levi's president and CEO Chip Bergh was outspoken against gun violence in 2018 and wrote an open letter asking gun owners not to bring firearms into their stores, offices or facilities.

In October 2018, Levi's reported its fourth consecutive quarter of double-digit revenue growth, putting it among the top performers in their industry.

Always political ever since it was first established in 1995, Lush is resolutely against animal testing and has backed campaigns involving causes that include Guantanamo prisoners, hunt saboteurs and anti-fracking campaigns.

This has helped it grow from a single store in Poole, Dorset, to more than 900 stores in just under 50 countries worldwide that generated sales of nearly £750m in 2017.

There is a risk that some people may not like it if you take a stand on something you care about.

There could be an even bigger risk from not doing or saying anything, and being seen as standing for nothing.

What do you and your customers care about?

Can you take an authentic stand on the issue?

What are you going to take a stand on?

YOU DON'T HAVE TO SAVE THE PLANET TO MAKE A DIFFERENCE

The world is facing many economic, societal and environmental problems.

As a result, customers are looking for ways to put their money to good use, in ways that matter for them, by spending their money with companies that they believe are making a difference to some of the problems that we face.

However, this trend is not just restricted to customers.

Employees too are starting to look for places to work where they can find meaning and purpose in the work that they do.

Therefore, a company's purpose and practices have emerged as a sustainable differentiator for both customers and employees.

The trap, however, that many organisations fall into when they think about building or developing a greater purpose, is that they jump to ideas that involve saving the planet or solving one of society's ills.

Purpose doesn't need to be grandiose. It can be local too as, ultimately, it is all about relevance and impact.

Take, TCC, for example, the largest Verizon Authorized Retailer in the USA. TCC empowered their employees to make a difference in their local communities through their Big Good initiative, where every quarter the employees of each store give back to a specific group of people (teachers, nursing homes, students and veterans).

Through their initiative, they learned that connecting with their customers and supporting the people and the community where they do business, at a hyper-local level, makes the most sense to them.

This helped them reduce staff turnover by 40%, make recruitment and training cost savings of around $5.7 mln per year and drive a rise in same store sales of 42% year on year. All this in an industry that is lucky to get low single digit annual sales percentage increases.

What are you doing to put purpose at the centre of your business?

Struggling?

If so, start by doing two things:

1. Find out what matters to your employees and customers, and

2. Figure out how you can help them matter.

ACHIEVE BALANCE
BY TAKING THE ROAD
LESS TRAVELED

Many customers want to use the new digital tools that brands are developing.

But, they are not adopting them at the rate that brands would like.

These same customers also often complain about the lack of the human touch in the experiences that brands are developing, and that they are regularly frustrated by their inability to speak to a real person when they encounter a problem that needs resolving.

Many brands are designing out human contact and defaulting to digital or technology-only solutions.

That's a mistake. A big one.

To rectify this situation, companies need to address a few key questions:

What is your experience strategy and why?

Is it high tech and low touch? Is it high touch and low tech? Is it low tech and low touch? Is it high tech and high touch?

Where is your experience now and how would you like it to develop over time?

How will it change for different types of customers?

Will it change depending on the stage of their journey?

Too few firms have considered these questions, and that might be one of the reasons behind why they are not getting the results they want from their customer experience efforts.

Now, there are no easy answers to these questions as it will require firms to make hard choices about what to do and, more importantly, what not to do.

Many firms won't do the work. And, will continue to be exasperated by the results that they get.

Others will, because they know that their customers are waiting.

As the poet, Robert Frost, said in his poem "The Road Not Taken":

"Two roads diverged in a wood, and I,
I took the one less traveled by,
And that has made all the difference."

Are you willing to answer the questions?

Make the choices?

And, do the work?

Spiderman's uncle, Ben, is recorded as giving the following piece of advice to the webbed avenger's alter-ego, Peter Parker:

"With great power, comes great responsibility."

That same piece of advice applies to many of the technological and scientific advances that have been made in recent years...

...our ability to 'nudge' people into action via advances in behavioural science

...our ability to 'hook' people into developing habit forming behaviours via advances in behavioural design

...our ability to build powerful algorithms and large data sets that power 'smart' products and services that make or recommend decisions for us

...our ability to track and coerce decisions, actions and behaviours with the advanced personalisation tools we have at our disposal.

Whilst it may seem like only a small thing to nudge a customer to do something, or design something to get them hooked, or use 'smart' algorithms to facilitate their decisions, leveraging these tools will have consequences. Their misuse can cause more damage than any additional value that they may create.

As result, companies would do well to not only exercise care and good judgement in how and when these new tools are applied and used, but also to decide how much is too much.

With these tools in hand, companies have a duty of care to their customers.

Are you prepared?

Do you have a set of standards, ethics, promises or guidelines that are actively managed and monitored?

Have you shared these with your customers?

Are you monitoring and managing the intended and unintended consequences of your use of these tools both for yourselves and your customers?

WITH
GREAT POWER,
COMES GREAT
RESPONSIBILITY

MAKING MUSIC

CX IS ABOUT MORE THAN F***ING METRICS!

Repeat after me:

CX is about more than f***ing metrics!
CX is about more than f***ing metrics!
(shouting) CX IS ABOUT MORE THAN F***ING METRICS!

It really is.

However, so much of the discussion around CX is dominated by metrics and data, and how we can improve our numbers, that it displaces everything else.

Including the customer.

Including innovation.

Including creativity.

Including _____
[feel free to fill in the blank]

Rory Sutherland sums up the organisational situation very well when he says:

"Unfortunately, it is often better to be measurably mediocre than immeasurably brilliant"

Are you guilty of making CX all about metrics in your organisation?

When you talk about customer experience in your organisation what do you talk about?

Where's the customer in your discussions?

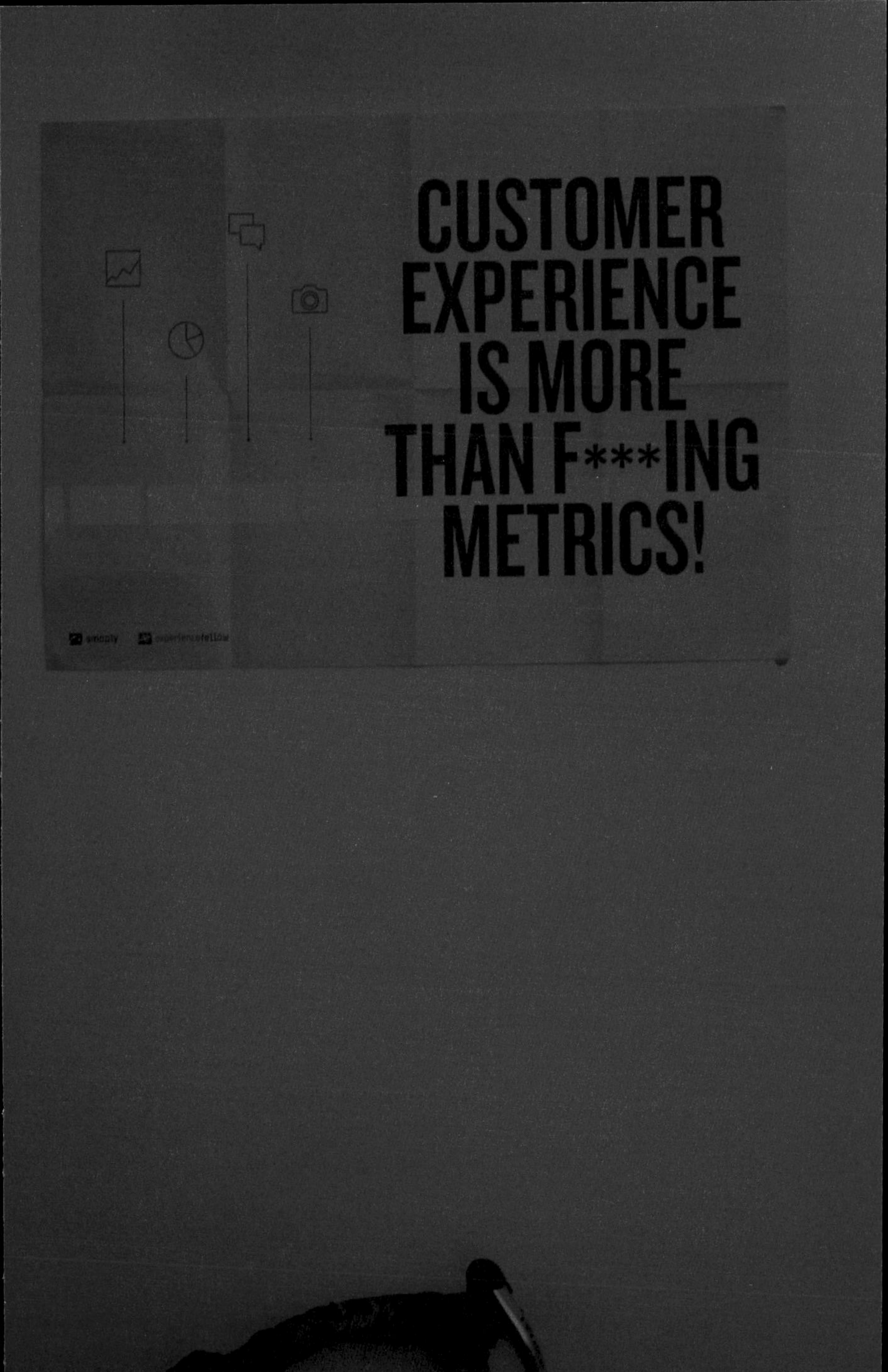

Source: Poster used by permission of www.morethanmetrics.com

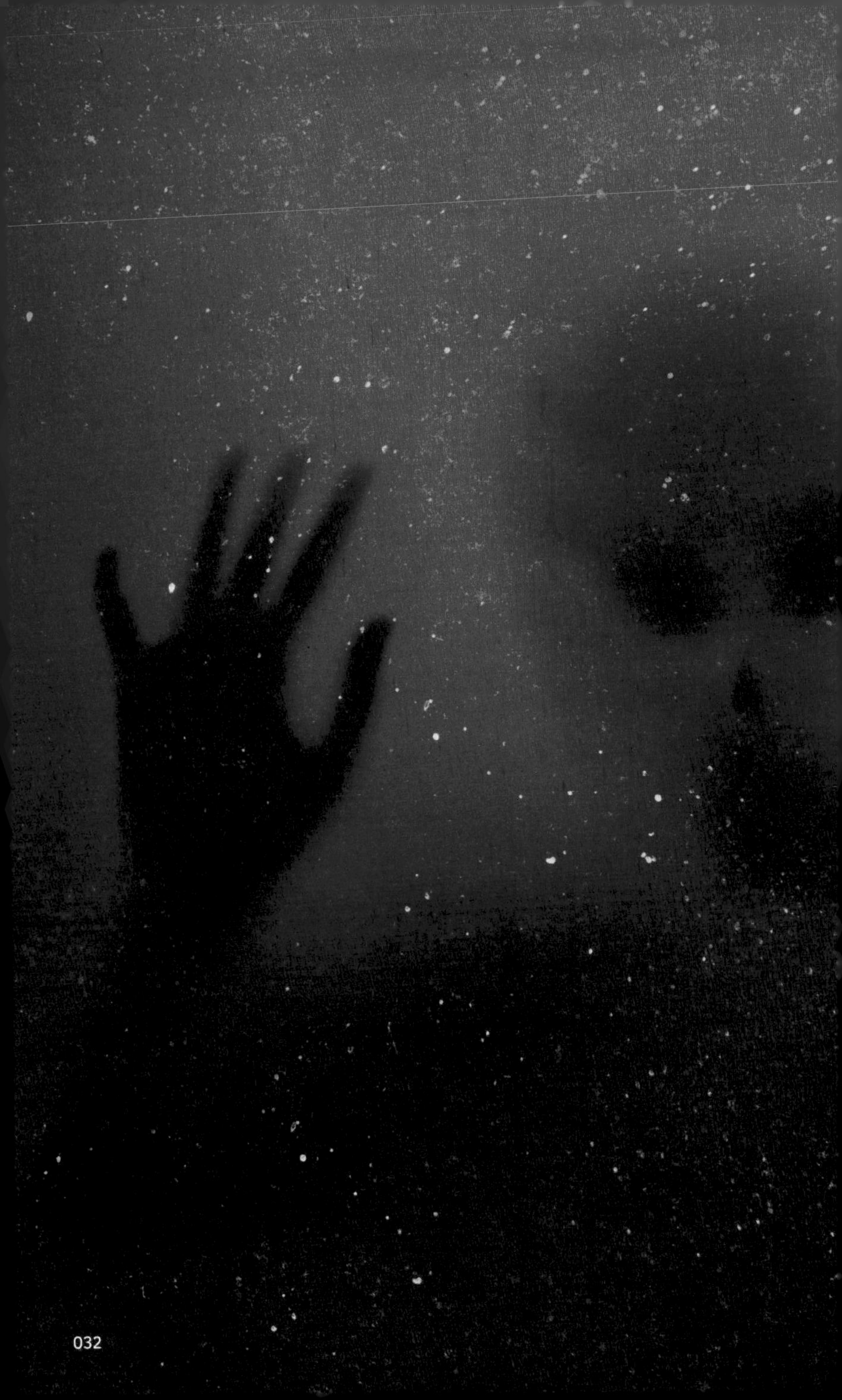

DON'T BE A CREEP!

Brands want to deliver personalised experiences for their customers.

Customers want personalised experiences too.

However, a large number (75%) of customers complain that most personalisation efforts are creepy.

Shockingly, many marketers (40%) also admit to finding elements of their own personalisation efforts creepy.

That runs counter to assertions by many brands that they care about their customers and that customer experience is a top priority for them.

What's going on?

Many marketers complain that they are hindered by insufficient and low-quality data.

Jascha Kaykas-Wolff, CMO of Mozilla, disagrees and reckons that the volume of data available to marketers is making them lazy.

Meanwhile, Jebbit, a technology firm that has pioneered a declared data approach, allows brands to deliver a personalised experience utilising no more than 3 or 4 good data points.

Boden in the UK, following their approach, has generated a 33-34% increase in their cart size and around a 52-53% higher conversion rate.

Alex Genov, Head of Customer Research at Zappos, goes further and believes that brands get sucked into the how (i.e., data and technology) and don't focus enough on the what (i.e., the experience they want to create).

By focusing only on the data, brands are in danger of not seeing the whole person, the context and, as a result, the whole opportunity.

How creepy are your personalisation efforts?

If you are in any doubt, please stop. Right now.

You need to start by defining what experience you want to deliver.

Ask yourself:

What is the absolute best journey my customer can take?

Are my personalisation efforts making that journey better?

What data do I need to achieve that?

GREAT AT A FEW OR
AVERAGE AT A LOT

In Dimension Data's 2017 Global Customer Experience Benchmarking Report they found that, on average, organisations are offering their customers a choice of nine different channels with which to engage with them. This number was forecast to rise to 11 channels over the course of 2018 and 2019.

That's a hell of a lot of channels.

What's more interesting is that only 8% of the organisations surveyed said that they have all of their channels connected. In fact, as many as 70% say that none or very few of their channels are connected, and 58% report that channels are still being managed in silos, with all of the data sharing and collaboration issues that come with that type of set up.

What's surprising is that if you think about the oft cited leading organisations when it comes to service and experience like Apple, Amazon, first direct, Zappos etc, and you count up how many channels they use to serve their customers, you will find that they only serve their customers over a handful of channels.

There's a lesson in there somewhere and I think it just might be:

It's better to be great at a few channels than average at a lot.

Right?

So, which channels are you going to decide to be great at?

And, which channels are you going to retire?

Make a kill list if you need to.

SIX RULES TO RULE ALL SURVEYS

Asking customers for feedback is an essential part of the improvement process for any business.

Most companies ask their customers for feedback and many customers are happy to provide feedback.

However, many companies suffer from low response rates and undo a lot of their good work through the way that they go about their surveys and feedback process.

To escape this trap, here's some things you should concentrate on when it comes to your own surveys.........

1. Make sure your survey is relevant to your customer,

2. Make sure it is short and the shorter it is the better,

3. Deliver it at the most appropriate point in their journey, this is kind of a big deal,

4. Let your customers tell you what they really think, and tell you in their own words,

5. Always thank them and let them know what you are doing with their feedback, it's rude not to,

6. And finally, don't survey them too much... it's annoying.

Do all of those things and you will be doing better than most.

How would you score yourselves on these six dimensions?

Work to do? Get to it.

STUDY YOUR OWN HISTORY

"In history, a great volume is unrolled for our instruction, drawing the materials of future wisdom from the past errors and infirmities of mankind." - Edmund Burke, Irish writer, politician, journalist and philosopher.

If you want to help your customers then you should study history.

I don't mean the sort of history that involves things like wars, empires and social strife.

The sort of history I believe you should be interested in is your own or, more specifically, your team's customer service or support history.

Here's why.

Recent research by Digital Genius found that a whopping 80% of customer service leaders responded that 20% of their tickets were highly repetitive, yet easy to resolve.

Moreover, over one-third (37%) of those leaders said that over 40% of their incoming tickets were highly repetitive, yet easy to resolve.

In addition, recent figures from Capgemini Odigo

CX UK found that 57% of customers call contact centers when they can't find what they are looking for online.

WTF? ALL of these tickets and calls are avoidable!!

They are ALL waste.

Just think of the time and effort wasted on all of those easy to resolve and simple tickets, the contacts that flow into the same agent queues, minute after minute, hour after hour, day after dreary day - each one of them begging for a good piece of content, some knowledge management, or an automation that will help those same agents focus on tackling more complex tasks & problems instead.

Brands, hello! Are you listening? Do you really care about your customers? Are you doing enough of the right things to make both your customers and your own lives easier?
Not on this evidence.
Study your own history.

Learn from it. Pronto.

Eliminate the repeat problems and, in doing so, watch your customer's and your employee's experience improve.

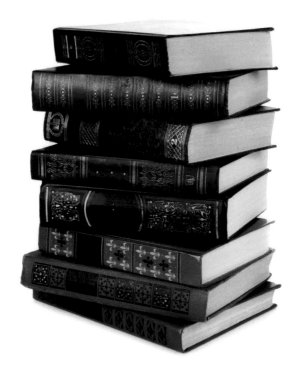

DOES YOUR BATHROOM SMELL?

Imagine you go to a restaurant that you have been looking forward to going to for a while, and the food and the service are great.

But, then you go to the bathroom and it is an unholy mess, and it really smells.

Now what do you think of the restaurant?

Does the cleanliness of the bathroom affect your perception of the overall experience?

Almost definitely.

Is the memory of your experience dominated by a recollection of that disgusting bathroom?

Probably.

Will it also have an impact on your propensity to recommend or return to that restaurant?

I think we all know the answer to this one...

Remember, customers will judge your expertise in areas they do not understand by your excellence in areas which they do.

So, are you looking at your experience in a holistic way?

Can you think of any 'smelly bathrooms' that exist in and spoil your experience?

The English electronic band, Depeche Mode, once wrote a lyric that said:

"It's a competitive world, Everything counts in large amounts."

The same is true of customer experience.

Most experience initiatives are dominated by the "new". New technology implementations, new digital initiatives, new revenue models. Etcetera.

However, these efforts tend to skew the focus of leadership away from some of the more mundane elements of a customer's experience, many of which are often seen as inconsequential.

Call these things grit, irritations, annoyances or sharp edges. Call them what you like.

But, these things matter to customers. A lot.

How many bits of grit or how many sharp edges can you identify in your service and customer experience?

What's causing them?

What are you doing about them?

How much progress are you making?

Could you do more?

Why aren't you doing more?

SWEAT THE SMALL STUFF

SIMPLICITY RULES, OK!

"Making the simple complicated is commonplace; making the complicated simple, awesomely simple, that's creativity."
- *Charles Mingus*

Our customers say that they want more choice.

But, when presented with more choice they often buy or do less than when they are presented with a smaller set of choices.

In 2000, psychologists Sheena Iyengar and Mark Lepper conducted a landmark experiment in a supermarket in California. When presented with a range of 24 jams, more shoppers stopped but only 3% went on to purchase a pot of jam. Meanwhile, when the display was changed to offer only 6 jams, whilst fewer shoppers stopped at the display 30% went on to buy a pot of jam.

It seems that whilst choice may be interesting to us, it is also confusing.

Companies that make things simpler and less confusing for their customers, and themselves, win big.

Since 2009 Siegel + Gale have been tracking the impact of 'simplicity' when it comes to brands. They have found that in an increasingly complex world, simplicity stands out when it comes to customer choice, service and experience. They have also found out that brands that focus on delivering simple service and experience deliver better results:

64% of customers will pay more for simpler experiences.

61% of customers are more likely to recommend a brand because it's simple.

A stock portfolio of the simplest global brands outperforms the major indexes by 330%.

62% of employees at simple companies are brand champions— versus only 20% of employees at complex companies.

Therefore, it seems that the reduction of choice and the quest for simplicity has value for not just customers but for employees and shareholders too.

It may not be easy to do. But… it's clear that simpler service and experience pays.

When was the last time you reduced the amount of choice you give your customers?

In other words, K.I.S.S.

"SIMPLICITY IS THE ULTIMATE SOPHISTICATION"
- Leonardo da Vinci

LAST IMPRESSIONS MATTER

When Pauline Wilson started her role as
Operations Director of Virgin Holidays, she
went undercover with her Marketing Director
on one of their own holidays, to experience
it through the eyes of their customers.

One of the biggest lightbulb moments from their trip
came when their customers kept telling them how
much they didn't like the last day of their holiday.

Not because they hadn't had a great holiday,
but more because after they had checked out
of their hotel they were left with time to kill and
little access to any facilities before heading
off to the airport to catch their flight home.

Overall, they felt forgotten, and that, after they
had checked out, the company had switched
its focus away from them to the new arrivals.

That was a real wake-up call for Pauline and her
colleague, and made them realise that the finish of
any experience is just as important as the start.

That insight helped them develop a new concept:
The Departure Beach - a dedicated Virgin Holidays
beach lounge at the hotel and, most importantly
still on the beach, that aims to help their customers
get the most out of the last day of their holiday.

Are you overlooking the end of your
customer's experience with you?

What could you do to make the end of
your customer's experience better?

The End

UNCONDITIONALLY YOURS

A few years ago my wife and I were on holiday in Havana, Cuba, and one evening, we found ourselves wandering around Old Havana looking for a place to go for dinner.

We stumbled across a funky looking bar/ restaurant called "Lamparilla Tapas Y Cerveza".

We didn't know anything about this restaurant (we didn't have any internet access) but it did look very interesting.

While perusing the menu out on the street, we were greeted by the host and whilst chatting away to her, Hana, my wife, jokingly asked if their food was any good.

The host was a little taken aback by this (obviously) but she confidently replied: 'If it isn't any good, then I'll pay'.

Her reply surprised us as it's not something that we've had said to us before. So, filled with optimism, we went inside and sat down to eat.

At the end of our meal, our host came over to our table again and asked us: "So, am I paying?"

We promptly answered 'No' and were delighted to be able to tell her that the food and service had been fantastic.

Our host offered us an unconditional service guarantee, so confident was she of the quality of their food and the experience that they delivered.

Do you offer an unconditional service guarantee?

If not, why not?

Do you not believe in your service enough to offer one?

What would it take for you to offer an unconditional service guarantee?

DO YOU DARE TO BE DIFFERENT?

Many companies and brands profess to want to be leaders in their field, or to stand out from the crowd.

But, when it comes down to it, they are not willing to do anything different, to take any risks or to try something new.

What happens is that they get bogged down with naval-gazing questions like: "What are the risks?", "What can go wrong?", "What will other people say?", "Where has this been done before?" and "Can we benchmark ourselves against our competition?"

All of which are recipes for mediocrity. The road to hell is paved with good intentions.

Sound familiar?

Do you want to lead and stand out?

Do you really?

Seriously?

Prove it.

Can you?

If not, what are you going to do about it?

I dare you.

EMBRACE THE ANGER, IT'LL MAKE THEM FEEL BETTER

From time to time things go wrong.

Sometimes badly.

And, customers complain.

But, most companies don't devote much time or effort to improving their complaints processes.

That's a little odd when you consider how many companies are utterly besotted with customer emotions at the moment.

Well guess what... complaints are all about emotions.

But, complaints deal with negative emotions, and that's hard work.

However, Mariana Alessandri, assistant professor of philosophy at the University of Texas-Pan American, suggests that complaining shouldn't be avoided, and can be a good thing. In an article at BigThink.com, she outlines how complaining allows customers to deal with, and process, many of the negative emotions that are associated with their complaint.

Indeed, doing so can also help make us feel better about the complaint and move past it.

So, don't avoid complaints or make it hard for your customers to complain.

Help and encourage them to complain so they can get their emotions off their chest.

It can help them feel better and may even improve their perception and memory of the 'experience' that they have had.

What do your customers complain about?

When was the last time you personally dealt with a complaint?

How did your customer feel when you had successfully dealt with their complaint?

MIND YOUR Ps AND Qs

The Bee Gees once sang:

"It's only words, and words are all I have to take your heart away".

Yet, many companies do not pay enough heed to the words that they use when communicating with their customers.

Think about your Terms & Conditions, your contracts, your cookie, privacy and data protection policies. Think about the many emails that your departments, especially complaints departments, send to customers.

Are they customer friendly? Are they easily understandable?

If not, what impact do they have on the customer's experience? And, what impact could changing them have?

Great Western Railways (GWR) in the UK decided to start operating under a principle of

"Real speak not rail speak".

Embarking on this journey, they quickly realised that they could not stop at rethinking how they communicated with customers but had to include their own supporting policies and procedures.

As a result, they took on the rewriting of over 200 internal documents, policies and procedures so that they were aligned with their goals and guiding principles.

Over the course of 6 quarters, they improved their NPS score by 29 points and reduced their customer effort score (CES) by 10 points. In addition, they also received a commendation from the regulator. No mean feat in the current UK rail environment.

The Bee Gees were right. Words matter. Not just the ones that we use to communicate with our customers but the words that are used to support us in doing that.

Are all of the words you use customer friendly?

Where are you going to start?

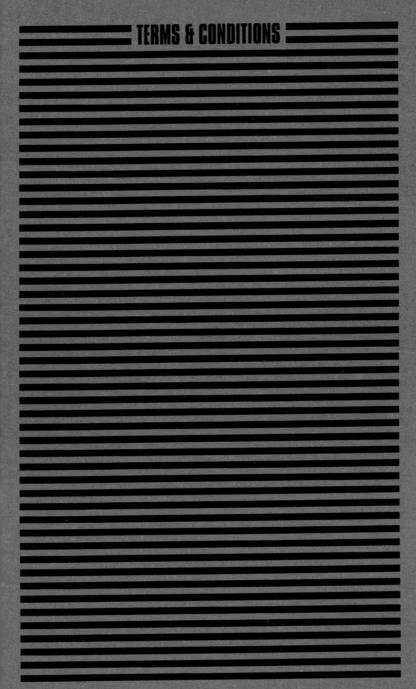

TERMS & CONDITIONS

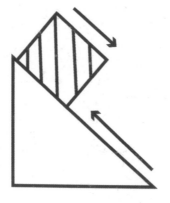

NOT ALL FRICTION IS BAD

There are a lot of folks that are saying that we should pursue a frictionless experience.

Not so fast.

Isn't there such a thing as good and bad friction?

Bad friction would be all of the things that are hard, uncomfortable, slightly irritating or inconsistent.

Good friction would be something that was quirky and unique to your brand, or an opportunity to engage or make an emotional connection.

So, do you really want to eliminate all of the friction in your customer's experience?

Some brands, like TK Maxx, embrace what people would normally classify as bad friction as being part of their experience.

In their advertising they say "Sure, it might feel a little haphazard in there but where else would you stumble on a designer dress while looking for a frying pan".

And, in a competitive market they are doing very well.

What would you classify as bad friction?

How are you going to eliminate that?

What would you classify as good friction?

How are you going to enhance that?

It's widely agreed that having happy and engaged employees directly contributes to an organisation's ability to deliver excellent service and experience.

This can be expressed as follows: good customer experience is a function of good employee experience, or to put it another way: $CX = f(EX)$

This is leading to a surge of interest in "employee journey mapping" as a way of developing and optimising the employee experience.

However, recent research by SAP Fieldglass shows that around 44% of workforce spend is on external talent. According to the study, over 65% of organisations need their external workforces to be able to operate at full capacity to meet customer demand, and to develop and improve products and services.

This is backed up by research from Deloitte, via their 2018 Global Human Capital Trends report, which shows that there is an emerging workforce ecosystem that is changing the way that organizations need to engage, attract and manage all types of workers.

Therefore, it is no longer good enough to just think about the employee experience, organisations need to start thinking about both the employee and external workforce experience if they are to deliver the experience that their customers desire.

So, our equation now looks like: $CX = f(EX + WX)$

Have you mapped out your employee experience and synced it with your customer's journey?

Have you included the broader worker experience?

Do you need to change that?

$$CX = f(EX + WX)$$

DWYS
YAGTD
WYSY
AGTDI

DWYSYAGTDWYSYAGTDI

DWYSYAGTDWYSYAGTDI is not a town in Wales!

DWYSYAGTDWYSYAGTDI is an acronym. Probably one of the biggest acronyms you have ever seen.

But, this mouthful of letters is also the bedrock of trust and credibility.

Figured it out yet?

It's very simple and to the point.

It stands for **"Do What You Say You Are Going To Do When You Say You Are Going To Do It"**

If you were to rate your business on its ability to DWYSYAGTDWYSYAGTDI, how would you score?

If you can confidently and comfortably say "all the time" then well done!

You are one of the few.

If not, then what are you going to do about it?

LESSONS FROM THE EDGE

The edges and the exceptions of your customers' experiences are where you really find out how good your service and your overall customer experience is.

In fact, I would go further and say that clues about your route to greatness lie in responding to, and being alive to, the edges and the exceptions.

Remember the over-booking incident involving Dr. David Dao, when he was violently dragged off a United Airlines plane in Chicago on the 9th of April 2017, losing two teeth and suffering a broken nose in the process?

You'd think that common sense would have prevailed. But, it didn't. Staff just followed procedure. And, it got ugly.

This brutal incident shows us that you only really know how good your experience and service is when it is tested in the crucible of extreme circumstances.

Not all of your policies will be customer-friendly 'in extremis', and that is where most of the big problems will lie.

Those scenarios may not happen very often, but when they do they can be very damaging.

Can you define a set of unlikely scenarios that could happen in your customer experience?

Can you use them to help you stress-test your policies and procedures?

Are you providing your staff with the right level of training and guidance to respond to these sorts of situations?

If not, does that not risk putting them in a compromising position?

Is that OK with you?

LOYALTY IS DEAD,
LONG LIVE LOYALTY

InMoment's 2018 *Retail CX Trends Report* contained the following quote from a customer:

"I'm treated with respect, and I'm not just a 'customer number' to them. They train their employees to care about me as a person, and they offer their best support when things don't go right. Even if things go wrong often, I won't change my loyalty to them because I can trust that they will always work with me to make things better and that they will always care for me as a loyal customer and friend."

The quote and the accompanying research in the report show that loyalty is not about loyalty programmes.

It's about consistency, respect, value and reliability.

Loyalty is a whole business game not just some bolted-on programme.

Are you relying too much on an indistinct loyalty programme to drive loyalty?

Should you be concentrating instead on making sure your customer's experience is more consistent, respectful, valuable and reliable?

What matters most to your customers… a loyalty points scheme to sit alongside the countless others, or consistently valuable, reliable and respectful service?

Should you be killing your loyalty programme so you can divert resources into consistency and reliability initiatives?

BRILLIANT AT THE BASICS

Many CX efforts are focused on surprising and delighting customers.

However, many of those are not delivering the desired results.

A better but less 'sexy' way is to focus on being brilliant at the basics. The basics that matter to your customers.

However, too few companies do this.

Ignoring the basics doesn't make sense from ANY angle. The financial and emotional RoI of helping customers avoid risk, failure, mistakes and disappointment is way higher than the RoI of any surprise or delight initiative.

Perhaps the reason behind this is that it is not easy work. It takes time, discipline and commitment.

But, it is worth it, and your customers are waiting.

Waiting for you to be brilliant at the basics.

What are your 'basics'?

What does 'being brilliant' at them mean to you and your customers?

How do you measure up?

Are you falling short?

What are you going to do about it?

BASICS!

THE WAY
WE ARE

IT'S ALL ABOUT THE CUSTOMER'S EXPERIENCE NOT CUSTOMER EXPERIENCE

What's the difference between "customer experience" and "the customer's experience"?

Literally, there are only four letters and an apostrophe's difference between the two terms, but in reality, the difference can be a "country mile".

Often when professionals and executives talk about customer experience the talk is dominated by talk of themes like share of wallet, metrics, personalisation, technology, artificial intelligence, data, analytics, yada yada.

That presents both a danger and a challenge to organisations that profess to being customer centric.

As customer experience becomes increasingly like any other functional specialism, the actual customer is in danger of getting lost and disembodied from the conversation.

Now, customer experience initiatives have to deliver benefits to an organisation by way of higher profits, increased revenues, cost savings, improved retention or better advocacy etc etc.

I get that.

But guess what... customer experience also has to embody the customer's experience. If not, then it is in danger of becoming just another function, process or system that does "things" to the customer.

In turn, it also then runs the risk of failing to live up to expectations and failing to deliver on its promise.

Just like what happened to CRM in its early days.

When you talk about customer experience what do you talk about?

When you talk about customer experience, have you forgotten the customer in that conversation? Where are they?

How can you make sure that they are always at the centre of the conversation?

Amazon leave an empty chair in every meeting to symbolise the customer. What are you going to do to put the customer at the centre of your conversations?

CULL YOUR METRICS

Coventry Building Society, a financial services institution in the UK, doesn't use sales incentive schemes or sales targets for any individual member of staff and haven't done since 2010.

Here's some other stats about them:

They have a savings growth that is twice the market rate and mortgage growth rate that is four times the market rate.

They are the most cost-efficient building society in UK.

They have the highest customer satisfaction of any major bank or building society.

They are ranked 1st for mortgages and savings by Fairer Finance.

They are one of the Sunday Times Top 100 companies.

92% of their staff say "I feel proud to work for this organisation"; and

97% of their staff say "This organisation can be trusted by its members".

Their lack of targets doesn't seem to be hindering their progress.

Interestingly, a study by Professor Jordan Etkin of Duke University, published in the Journal of Consumer Research in 2016, called The Hidden Cost of Personal Quantification, found that whilst measuring an activity can increase how much of the activity we do, at the same time it can it also reduce our enjoyment of and engagement with that activity.

How many metrics are you monitoring on a daily, weekly, monthly basis?

How many of them really tell you how you are doing and how many are for vanity purposes? Be honest.

How many could be classed as over-measurement and could be having a negative impact on performance or the quality of outputs?

Which of them really tell how you, your employees and your customers are doing?

Time to cull some of your metrics?

074

ZIG ZIGLAR WAS SPOT ON!

Many customer experience professionals struggle to build relevance and impact in large organisations.

They should read Zig Ziglar's book See You At The Top.

In it, he wrote:

"You will get all you want in life, if you help enough other people get what they want."

This was brought to life by a participant at an Econsultancy roundtable on "Effective leadership in the Digital Age" that clearly understood this strategy when they said:

"I developed a strategy of digital by stealth. I looked for manageable projects that were other people's problems and I helped deliver a digital answer. It's amazing the goodwill you can build quickly when you make other people look good."

By the way, it doesn't just work for digital or inside organisations.

It works with customers too.

What do your customers really want?

What do your colleagues really want?

Are you really helping them get what they want, what they really really want?

Sheldon Yellen, the CEO of BELFOR Holdings, Inc, a global disaster relief and property restoration company, personally writes a birthday card to every one of Belfor's 7,400 employees every year.

Think about that. That works out, on average, to be over 30 cards every working day of the year and he's being doing it for the last 30 odd years.

That's some effort.

And, that's the amount of effort that he's willing to put in to show his employees that he cares.

In 2018 on his 60th birthday he received a hand-written birthday card from every one of Belfor's employees.

Now, the biggest problem he has is where to put all of his birthday cards!

Do you care about your employees and your customers?

How much?

What are you doing to demonstrate that?

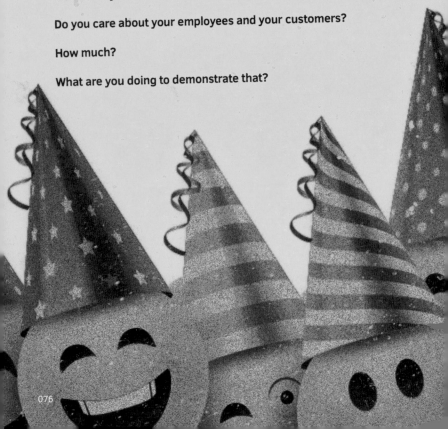

HOW MUCH DO YOU CARE?

LIVE TO SERVE

In his latest book *The Excellence Dividend* Tom Peters wrote the following:

**Organizations exist to serve.
PERIOD.
LEADERS LIVE TO SERVE.
PERIOD.
SERVICE is a beautiful word.
SERVICE is character, community, commitment. (And profit.)
SERVICE is not "Wow".
SERVICE is not "raving fans".
SERVICE is not "a great experience".
SERVICE is "just" that – SERVICE.**

Tom nailed it with that short passage.

Real service is a calling, a journey and a passion.

But, some people have a problem with service or the idea of serving.

In a conversation with Seth Godin about his latest book *This Is Marketing* he told me he believes that many people get caught up with thinking that service and serving is about subservience.

It's not.

It's about much more than that. Look at some of the greatest leaders of our time - Mandela, Gandhi, Patton - they were all in service to their people.

Moreover, he believes a lot of this can be traced back to our worldview and whether we think that life is a zero-sum game or not.

So, what's your worldview?

And, what is your relationship to the word service and what it means to serve?

Be honest.

Personally, I am proud to live a life of service.

Are you?

If so, who are you serving?

And, who (or what) are you in service to?

EMPATHY IS NOT SOFT,
IT'S HARD

"O wad some Power the giftie gie us, To see oursels as ithers see us!" - *Robert Burns - To A Louse*

Everyone is talking about how having more empathy for customers can lead to the delivery of better service and experiences.

So, why do some companies get it wrong and others get it right?

Researchers at Pennsylvania State University and the University of Toronto recently conducted a study that produced a clue.

They found that empathy is hard work. And, because of that people tend to avoid being empathetic because of just that: the hard work involved.

Some dismiss empathy as being touch feely nonsense and a bit soft.
But, in reality, empathy is hard work.

The most empathetic companies hire the right people and the best people.

The most empathetic companies hang out with their customers.

The most empathetic companies require their people to be their customers too, even if only for a little while so they can live the experience they are to be part of.

The most empathetic companies conduct empathy building exercises.

All of which can be hard work and take time.

Do you want to improve the empathy you have for your customers?

How hard are you willing to work?

What are you willing to do to achieve that?

Where are you going to start?

When are you going to start?

081

GET YOUR HANDS DIRTY

I imagine that everyone has seen the TV show: Undercover Boss.

Most of the participants on the show are aghast at the things they see, the inadequacies of many of the systems and processes they have put in place, and how wonderful many of the people that serve customers are.

However, how many senior leaders in organisations go through this type of experience?

Not many. And certainly not enough.

Why not?

Imagine if everyone in a company served customers in store or fielded support calls or answered customer emails or did something like that or a regular basis.

Imagine the insights and new understanding that could be gained.

Imagine, if done well, how many extra support or service hours it could deliver.

Imagine the impact it could have on the morale of your front-line employees.

Just, imagine.

Too busy? Not the best use of your time?

Really? I thought you were better than that.

What better use of your time is there than serving, helping and understanding your customers and employees?

When is the next time you are going to get your hands 'dirty'?

I made up a law:

THE LAW OF
THREE SHITS

The original version states:

Do good shit,
Keep doing good shit and
Shit will take care of itself.

A friend suggested an alternative version:

Do good shit,
Ignore the shit-sayers and
Shit will take care of itself.

One deals with lack of discipline and commitment and the ability to be relentless in the pursuit of "doing good shit".

The other speaks to the social phobia that haunts many organisations, i.e., caring too much about what other people will think.

Which law of three shits, if any, applies to you and your organisation?

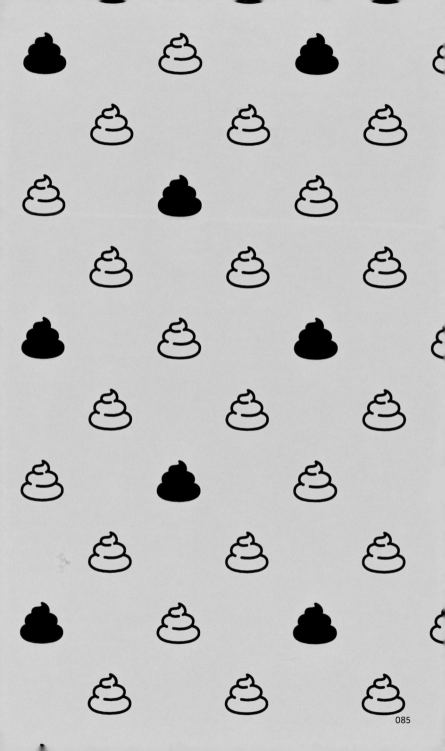

ARE YOU RESTLESS

AND RELENTLESS?

I remember watching an interview with Buddy Guy, the famous American blues guitarist and singer.

In it he talked about his relationship with his father, and some advice he received from him early in his career.

His father's advice to him was:

"Don't be the best in town, son. Just try to be the best until the best come around."

For me that quote beautifully captures want it takes to be the best.

It requires a focus on ourselves and how good we can be in the knowledge that it may only be temporary.

Most of the leading lights in customer experience, the brands that are perennially held up as inspirations and something to aspire to, don't talk about being the best or number one.

In fact, they don't talk that much at all about customer experience.

They are both restless and relentless in their pursuit of doing the right things and the best things for their customers.

Are you?

What does being the best mean for you?

What does being the best mean for your organisation?

What does being the best mean for your customers?

What does being the best mean for your colleagues?

BE MORE BRIAN CLOUGH!

My friend, James Lawther, told me a story once about Brian Clough, the legendary Nottingham Forest football manager. After he took over in 1976, Clough set about transforming this ordinary team into Division Two champions in 1977, Division One title winners in 1978, and European champions in 1979 and 1980.

The story concerned what he is said to have done when the team suffered an away loss.

On the way back from losing a match, he is said to have routinely stopped the team bus at a pub on the way back home and to have told the players something like:

'You are all adults and you all know what went wrong. Now, go and have a beer, get the loss out of your system and let's move on from it so that we can focus on winning our next game'.

These types of approaches are quite common in sport.

But, I'm not sure that we can say the same about business.

In many organisations, when something goes wrong there is a high likelihood that it will prompt a lengthy and, quite possibly, forensic investigation into the what, the why, the who and the how of the whole matter.

Now, whilst it's important to learn lessons from when things go wrong, there is a danger that focusing too heavily on what went wrong rather than on what went right creates a culture that focuses on not losing, rather than on one that focuses on winning.

This, in turn, can have a devastating impact on employee motivation and engagement.

What happens in your organisation when things go wrong?

Are you endanger of focusing on not losing rather than winning? Can you tell the difference between these two approaches?

Could your approach be undermining your engagement efforts?

What do you do when things go right?

DEAR CEO

LONDON BUSINESS SCHOOL, IN THEIR 2017 BUSINESS LEADERS SURVEY, FOUND THAT OF ALL THE SENIOR EXECUTIVES THAT THEY SPOKE TO **NEARLY 60% REPORTED REGULAR CONFLICT AND IN-FIGHTING** WITHIN THE SENIOR TEAM, AS EACH C-SUITE EXECUTIVE PURSUED THEIR OWN AGENDA.

NOW, IF SENIOR EXECUTIVES ARE NOTICING THIS ABOUT THEMSELVES, THEIR OWN ORGANISATIONS, THEIR COLLEAGUES AND THEIR OWN SENIOR TEAM THEN YOU CAN BE PRETTY SURE THAT EVERYONE ELSE IN THEIR ORGANISATIONS WOULD HAVE NOTICED THESE PROBLEMS TOO.

SO, HOW CAN EMPLOYEES BE EXPECTED TO BE MORE ENGAGED AND WORK MORE EFFECTIVELY TOGETHER TOWARDS THE COMMON GOAL OF DELIVERING GREAT SERVICE AND EXPERIENCE WHEN THEY SEE IN-FIGHTING AND CONFLICT WITHIN THEIR SENIOR TEAM?

WHILE EVERY MEMBER OF THE C-SUITE HAS THEIR PART TO PLAY, ULTIMATELY IT IS YOUR TEAM AND YOUR RESPONSIBILITY TO MAKE SURE THAT EVERYONE IS ALIGNED, FOCUSED AND PULLING IN THE SAME DIRECTION.

PLEASE. SORT. IT. OUT.

YOUR PEOPLE AND YOUR CUSTOMERS ARE WAITING.

YOURS,

[Sign your name and send]

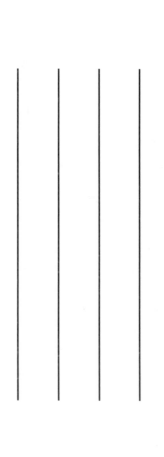

AFFIX
STAMP
HERE

WHEN WAS THE LAST TIME YOU WENT TO THE GEMBA?

The Japanese word "gemba" means the real place or the place where something really happens.

In Japan, police detectives talk about the "scene of the gemba" and news reporters talk about "reporting from the gemba."

The word implies that a better understanding of something can only be achieved by going to the place where it occurs.

Toyota and its managers having been "going to the gemba", the factory floor in their case, since the 1950s to help them gain a better understanding of what is and is not working.

Now, the "gemba" will mean different things to different businesses.

For Andrew Lawson, Chief Product Officer of online personal finance peer-to-peer lending company Zopa.com, that means inviting customers into their offices to observe them going through the actual experience of investing or withdrawing money or taking out a loan.

Peter McGuinness, CMO of yogurt company Chobani, requires that every member of his demand team gets out into the market every two weeks to walk stores, and to speak to customers and dairy category managers.

Meanwhile Martijn Gribnau, Chief Transformation Officer, at Genworth Financial, and a veteran of large transformation programmes at ING and IPSoft, the gemba is part of every new role, and a daily practice. When he starts in an organisation he always starts as an intern so he gets to see all of the primary processes and how things are really working. That way he gets a better idea of what is doable. Following that, Martijn spends a third of his time with his own employees, a third just walking around getting a better understanding of the business, and the rest of his time with other work.

So, where is your gemba?

One thing is for sure, whether you go to it or bring it to you there is value, difference, motivation and insight in going to the gemba on a regular basis.

When was the last time you were there?

What did you learn?

When are you going again?

現場

DO YOU DARE TO BE DIFFERENT?

Long have we heard stories told about the death of the bookstore.

Despite this, some creative businesses are being defiant in the face of these stories.

Morioka Bookstore in the Ginza district of Tokyo has only one book title for sale at any one time. They pick one book, have multiple copies in stock, offer it for sale for one week only, and organise a series of events around the book to allow readers to better connect with the book and the author.

Elizabeth's Bookshops are the largest second-hand bookshop chain in Australia and they started their "Blind Date With a Book" initiative a few years ago, where they carefully select a number of different books across a range of different categories, and then they gift wrap the book and write a short description of it on the wrapping paper. Their approach adds a degree of mystery and surprise to the overall book buying and reading experience, but also an element of trust. Trust that the book store knows about books and knows what they are doing.

Bunkitsu, another bookstore, has recently opened in Tokyo, and charges a cover charge (roughly $13) for entrance. Inside the minimal space made up of concrete and wood, you find a curated and beautifully organised collection of 30,000 books and magazines that you are free to wander around with your free cup of coffee or tea. Spend an hour or two or all day there. Buy what you find or peruse endlessly. It's up to you. This bookstore is more like an art gallery or a museum than it is a traditional bookstore.

These examples show that despite the very competitive nature of their particular markets, they are not engaging in a race to the bottom like many of their competitors.

These three companies show what can be done with a bit of creativity, some self-belief and a lot of guts.

They dare to be different.

Do you?

How?

Prove it.

WHEN WAS THE LAST TIME
YOU SUCKED AT SOMETHING?

**"DUDE, SUCKING AT SOMETHING IS THE FIRST
STEP TOWARDS BEING SORTA GOOD AT SOMETHING!"**
- Anon
(seen painted on a telecoms cabinet at the edge of Churchill Square, Brighton, UK, 2017)

To suck at something means that
you have tried something new.

It's also likely that you have taken a risk,
failed and have learnt something.

Many people talk about being more agile
or having an agile organisation.

But, when was the last time that you, you
personally, could say that you sucked at
something?

Even a little thing?

A thing that you did for your customer
or for your colleagues?

If you can't then how are you learning?

How are you getting better?

DUDE
SUCKIN AT SOMETHING IS THE FIRST STEP TOWARDS BEING SORTA GOOD AT SOMETHING!

Don't be a pointy head

Traditionally, specialism and expertise have been central to an individual's success and career advancement.

However, ever increasing specialism and expertise can also lead to narrow and blinkered thinking.

And, a rise in "pointy headism".

Pointy heads are more concerned with (and have greater loyalty to) their own function, department or team than any overall brand or organisational purpose.

In this increasingly complex, competitive and connected world, pointy headed people are not helpful. In fact, they can be hugely annoying and downright obstructive.

What we need are more systems thinkers... professionals that see beyond their specialisms, their expertise and their functions, and appreciate how everything they do is connected to (and has an impact on) other people and things.

Are you a pointy head?

Do you really understand the intended and unintended consequences of the work that you do, or the decisions you make?

Do you really?

Seriously?

So, how do they impact your customers and employees?

Now that you really see the impact that you have, what will you do as a result?

In his Recalibrate (2017) stand-up comedy show, Russell Howard told a story about some words of wisdom that he received from his Dad.

They ended with the following words:

"Do your best and don't be a dick."

How would you score on a 'dickometer' if you applied that code to how you treat your customers, your employees, your peers and your suppliers?

Should that, or a variant of it, be your new 'modus operandi'?

You're welcome.

DO YOUR BEST AND

DON'T BE A DICK

FOR PUNKS
EVERYWHERE

employee engagement fuels better levels of service, a more engaging customer experience and better business results.

However, consider these pieces of research:

Gallup found that a whopping 70% of the variance between top quartile and bottom quartile

THE MIDDLE

performing companies can be explained by the quality of that organisation's managers.

Bas Koene at Rotterdam School of Management and Behnam Tabrizi at Stanford University's Department of Management Science and Engineering found, in separate pieces of research, that middle management plays a prominent role in successful change programmes and, thus, competitive firms.

Meanwhile, Bersin by Deloitte's 2014 Leadership Development Factbook shows that first-level managers each receive, on average, only 34% of the leadership development funding that emerging/high potential leaders receive and around 20% of the amount that senior leaders receive.

First level and middle management should not

MATTERS

be forgotten and play a huge part in making firms competitive, and allowing them to deliver the service and experiences that customers demand.

Like in a sandwich, the filler is just as important as the bread.

Are you neglecting your middle managers?

Could that be the thing that is holding you back?

STEAM
not
STEM!

Education policy in recent years has focused heavily on developing skills in STEM subjects: Science, Technology, Engineering, and Mathematics, in response to our heavily computerised age.

However, two things are becoming clear

Most people don't write code for a living, and empathy and being able to develop a meaningful connection with customers is becoming increasingly important.

As a result, many firms have hired a lot of technically brilliant people but are struggling with building empathetic connections with their customers.

Jamf is a provider of software for enterprises and smaller businesses that helps them manage their Apple devices. They have around 700 employees and over 12,000 customers around the globe. Jamf found that when they focused on hiring people with the right sort of skills they needed—emotional intelligence, empathy, authenticity, joyfulness, passion, technical curiosity and aptitude—they ended up with more than 60% of employees holding a liberal arts degree, as opposed to a computer science or other technical degree.

One of Jamf's founders is quoted as saying at a management meeting: "We are trying to solve problems that didn't exist yesterday and that's what a liberal arts education gives you".

What they found is that...

Training technical skills is faster and easier than training empathy.

Liberal arts graduates have often already developed empathy musculature.

Liberal arts education seems to focus on how to learn.

Want to develop an empathetic connection with your customers?

Is it time for you to evaluate your approach to talent?

Is it time for a **STEAM (Science, Technology, Engineering, Arts and Mathematics)** approach?

After all, art informs science, technology, engineering, and

CHEERS FOR PEERS

TINYpulse, an employee engagement platform, have a really popular feature they call Cheers for Peers.

What happens with this feature is that employees can send 'cheers' or kudos to clients, prospects, peers and co-workers to thank them for a job well-done, a bit of help provided, a new piece of business or something like that.

What a great little thing.

From time to time we need little reminders of what it means to be human, that we are social beings and everyone likes a bit of recognition from time to time.

Unfortunately, in the maelstrom of modern business life these gestures often get forgotten.

Or, they don't often get repeated.

So, who amongst your peers deserves a 'Cheers' from you today?

How are you going to deliver your 'Cheers'?

Will it be face to face, via hand-written card, small gift, email, text message, phone or video call?

Which medium will have the most impact? Why?

How are you going to make sure this is not a one-time thing?

How will you recruit your colleagues to start doing the same thing?

What's the best way to scale this practice across your whole organisation?

FRONTLINE

SUPER HEROES

It's a perennial wonder to me that the majority of the people that actually serve customers are often some of the lowest paid, under-equipped and least respected of all employees in any organisation.

Those employees play an essential brand ambassador role at crucial times in the customer's journey, whether that is at the point of service, sale or help when something goes wrong.

And yet, they often work for organisations that profess to being customer obsessed or customer centric.

How does that make sense?

Moreover, these roles are evolving, and are doing so rapidly. As higher levels of self-service and the utilisation of artificial intelligence, chat bots and other tech applications take hold, these roles are now starting to require a deeper level of thinking, empathy and problem-solving skills.

However, there is still a bit of a negative stigma in many business circles around the profession of customer service or support.

The largest majority of folks that work in customer service and support are passionate about their work. And guess what, they love helping people.

Don't you think it is time that we start treating them like the heroes they are?

Do you?

THE ANSWERS ARE RIGHT
IN FRONT OF YOU

A friend of mine, Joel Bailey, told me a story about Lloyds, a UK bank, who were in the process of redesigning their mortgages.

To do that they assembled a data team to gather and analyse a whole heap of customer and operational data so that they could identify the top problems that customers faced.

While they were going about their business, one bright spark gathered a bunch of front-line agents together, got them into a room, and told their supervisors to bugger off for a while so they could speak freely. She gave them tea, coffee and a bunch of doughnuts and in 30 minutes they were able to identify the top 10 problems that their customers faced.

Six weeks and hundreds of hours later the data analysis team returned and presented their results only to find that the front-line agents were 80% right.

So, are you willing to wait six weeks and use up hundreds of hours and many thousands of pounds or dollars to be 100% right? Or would you rather invest 30 minutes and a tray of doughnuts to be 80% right?

The answers you need are right in front of you. You only have to go, ask, and (here is the really important bit) listen!

EE, in their UK mobile business, did a similar thing. They listened to their customers and their frontline staff and fixed what they said was broken. In doing so they reduced their customers propensity to call by 88% over two years, and increased their NPS and eNPS scores by 21 and 57 points respectively over a similar period.

What the hell are you waiting for?

SEARCHING FOR PASSION

The role of front-line customer service staff is evolving.

Technology is allowing organisations to eliminate many of the mundane and repetitive parts of their jobs, freeing them up to focus on solving more complex customer issues as well as developing deeper emotional connections with customers.

As a result, front-line agents that have higher-levels of communication, empathy and problem-solving skills, as well as the sort of passion that is contagious, are in increasing demand.

The problem is that traditional methods of recruitment are not great at identifying these sorts of skills.

As a result, some companies are responding with creative recruitment methods to help them find staff with a passion for service.

Wayfair recruits at local Comic-Con events and runs an Escape Room challenge.

Lyft uses a mixer/speed dating type recruitment method.

Citizen M, operates 'Casting Days' (modelled on theatre & film casting days) when they are looking to hire new "Hotel Brand Ambassadors".

Voxpro, who provide customer support to brands like Airbnb, Nest, Google & SuperCell, use AI-powered testing to gauge how receptive potential employees are to continuous change, and their ability to deliver what they call 'beautiful customer experiences'.

So, if you want to hire the sort of people that are going to deliver a stand out experience for your customers, how creative are you being?

Where are you going to look to find the passion and the skills that you are searching for?

What are you going to try?

FANS, FANS, FANS

CHECK YOUR ASSUMPTIONS

In Powerhouse: Insider accounts into the world's top high-performance organizations, Brian MacNeice, one of the co-authors, tells a story about visiting a school during a trip to Finland, where they saw a class of 9-year olds studying Maths.

Outside of the class they saw two young boys sitting at desks in the corridor.

Brian asked the Headteacher what the boys had done to be excluded from class.

The Headteacher laughed and said that they had done nothing wrong and had chosen to sit outside the class as they like to discuss and debate things when they are problem-solving and to do this inside the class would be disruptive.

This story clearly illustrates the assumptions that we make based on our own experiences and how wrong they can be.

The American actor, Alan Alda, in a commencement address at his daughter's college captured it best when he said:

"Your assumptions are your windows on the world. Scrub them off every once in a while, or the light won't come in."

When was the last time that you listed out or examined the assumptions you make, especially the ones about yourself, your team-mates, your employees, your bosses and your customers?

Assumptions like....

Customers won't pay for better service

Customers want more choice rather than less

Millennial customers want digital solutions only and don't want to talk to people

All of which are untrue.

What assumptions are you making about your customers?

WE ALL LOVE A PRAT

Richard Shotton wrote a book called The Choice Factory: 25 Behavioural Biases That Influence What We Buy.

In it, he describes a behavioural bias called "The Pratfall Effect" that was first articulated by Elliot Aronson, Professor of Psychology at Harvard, who found that people (and brands) that admit or exhibit a flaw tend to be more appealing.

In his classic experiment, Aronson recruited a friend to take part in a quiz. However, beforehand he gives the friend the answers to the quiz and at the time of the quiz the friend gets around 90% of the answers right and wins by miles.

But then, as he is standing up at the end of the quiz he makes a 'pratfall', a small blunder. In this case, he spills a cup of coffee down himself.

This is all recorded.

Aronson then takes the recording and he plays two versions to people. They either see the entire performance including the pratfall or they just see the quiz performance.

Aronson found that people said that the contestant who made a mistake was significantly more appealing than the one who gave the near perfect performance.

The implication being that the closer that we get to perfection the less believable we can become.

Many brands have used The Pratfall Effect over the years....

Can you name them?

What flaws do you have?

Be honest.

Rather than covering them up, how can you turn your flaws to your advantage?

HIGH SCORE

PLEASANT

THERE'S WHAT HAPPENS AND THEN THERE'S WHAT WE MAKE IT MEAN

Can we design emotion into a customer's experience?

No.

There's the experience that we design and then there is what customers make it mean based on how they interpret it.

That's it.

We have no control over the prior experiences of our customers, their culture, their character, their context, their perspective, their values etc.

Trying to design exact emotions into a customer's experience is a fool's errand. We cannot control how a customer will feel about something.

The only thing we can control is what we do and how we do it.

Dr. Simon Moore, a Chartered business and consumer psychologist, who specialises in uncovering emotional and personality influences on behaviour, agrees. He explains it really well when he says that the best thing that a brand can do is "be more pleasant to people", and "if you can increase your 'pleasant score' you are more likely to be successful."

That does not mean that we should not spend time both building a better understanding of our customers and monitoring how they feel about what we do and how we do it.

Not at all.

But, we should be clear about what we can control and what we can't.

Start by asking yourself: How pleasant is the experience of our customers?

Is it pleasant enough?

If not, what needs to change?

Smash your pleasant score.

CUSTOMERS ARE HELPFUL, SOMETIMES

Collaborating with customers, co-creating new products and services is very fashionable at the moment.

But, does it work and is it a good idea?

Apparently, it depends...

Building on the work of his peers, Rotterdam School of Management's Professor Jan van den Ende and a couple of his colleagues studied 132 recent innovation projects by Dutch firms to find an answer.

In their study they differentiated between utilitarian innovations, i.e., those that create new functionality or involve new/improved technology, and hedonic innovations, i.e. those that are designed to evoke a sensory or emotional experience, or that have a large degree of a personal identity/expression attached to them.

What they found was that involving customers in a product/service development process is a good idea when the innovations are utilitarian in nature and, in particular, when the innovations are more radical in nature. And, when firms do this it tends to lead to greater market success.

However, involving customers in the product development process for hedonic innovations can actually decrease the chances of market success due to the social process/dynamics that exist around such innovations, i.e., what people think, are other people doing/wearing this, what does this say about me, etc.

Therefore, if your innovation is going to be utilitarian in nature then get your customers involved, ask their opinion, ask them what new features or functionality they would like to see.

But, if your innovation is likely to be more hedonic in nature then don't get your customers involved straight away. Instead, be design led, build some prototypes and test them out to see if they will work or not.

Are you organising your innovation activity along utilitarian and hedonic lines?

Are you getting your customers involved in your innovation process?

With this insight in mind, are you making mistakes?

A NOTE OF CAUTION

Here's another story from Richard Shotton's book *The Choice Factory* (it's really good, you should buy it!). In this one he cites an experiment conducted by Adrian North, a University of Leicester psychologist, where North played different music in the wine aisle of a local supermarket every week, i.e., one week they played German music and the next week they played French music.

He was interested in the effect of music on French and German wine sales.

When French music was played 77% of the French or German wine that was sold was French.

Conversely, when German music was played 73% of the wine sold was German.

However, what was interesting was that when he stopped people who had bought wine, and asked them why they had chosen that particular wine, only 2% of people spontaneously mentioned the music.

Moreover, 86% of them flat out denied that the music had any effect on them whatsover.

This story does a great job of illustrating David Ogilvy's famous quote:

"Consumers don't think how they feel. They don't say what they think and they don't do what they say".

Customers are often quixotic in nature.

However, that is the challenge that lies at the heart of understanding them, earning their trust, loyalty and advocacy.

Are you up for it?

Let's go.

DEMOS & B-SIDES

THE BEST OF YOU

Most people would agree that if you have happy and engaged employees it's easier to deliver great service and a better customer experience.

However, to accomplish that most firms tend to invest in better training, a nicer office environment and all sorts of other perks and benefits.

One CEO thinks that those things are necessary but they are not sufficient, and believes that engagement and happiness are not limited to what happens at work, but are also impacted by other external factors like bills, rent, mortgage payments, childcare and travel costs etc.

That CEO is Dan Price of Gravity Payments in Seattle who implemented a new minimum salary of $70,000 for all employees back in 2015, after reading a 2010 paper by Princeton scholars, Daniel Kahneman and Angus Deaton. They found that emotional well-being rises with income but that "there is no further progress beyond an annual income of ~$75,000".

In doing so, he wanted to remove many of the life barriers that his employees faced so that they could bring the best versions of themselves to work.

Six months after the launch of the initiative, the number of new leads coming into the business had grown from 30 to 2,000 inquiries per month, they had received thousands of new job applicants (no surprise there), profits had doubled, employee retention had soared and client retention had grown from its already high base of 91% to 95%. The industry average client retention rate is 68%.

Now, if Dan Price is willing to make that sort of change to his business…

What more could you and your organisation be doing to help your employees bring the best version of themselves to work?

What would need to happen to make that come about?

When and where are you going to start?

CONSTRAINTS DRIVE
CREATIVITY

We now live in an always-on, always-connected, 24/7/365 world.

And, to compete in such a world, a company needs to have a real-time omni-channel presence, where it constantly monitors, matches and meets the ever-changing needs of its customers.

Right?

Well, that seems to be the prevailing wisdom.

But... isn't there a problem with that? If everyone is trying to do more and more to become better and better does it not, at some point, become harder and harder to stand out from the crowd?

If so, then surely the question has to be not "how do we do more" but "how do we do things differently in order to stand out"?

"The worst thing you can do is give a creative person a blank sheet of paper" - *Unknown source*

To achieve that sometimes we need to create constraints in order to drive better outcomes.

For example, Stephan Aarstol, Founder & CEO of Tower Paddle Boards in San Diego, implemented a 5-hour work day as he was concerned about his employees well-being and their productivity.

This new regime had no impact on their salaries, and Stephan fully expected to take a 40% hit from their customers.

However, in reality, they experienced no negative impact from their customers as they self-adjusted to the new opening hours, and the hours that the Tower team were available to help.

In fact, a year after introducing this new way of working, their revenues had gone up 42% and profitability was north of 30%.

What happened was that the 5-hour workday forced Tower employees to communicate and operate more effectively and efficiently - amongst themselves and with their customers.

This goes to show that putting constraints on things can often force a creative solution.

What constraints are you placing on your people to generate better outcomes or drive more creativity?

DO YOU HAVE INDIGESTION?

Apparently as many as 70% of all digital, customer experience and large change and transformation programmes fail or fail to meet their primary objectives.

Moreover, speak to business executives and leaders and almost all of them are in the midst of some sort of change project at any given time.

In fact, many are in the midst of more than one at any given time.

Indigestion is normally associated with having eaten too much or difficulty in digesting something. Is it possible that many of these programmes fail not due to faults with the programmes themselves but due to corporate indigestion?

Perhaps the lessons from our own biology are that (a) we shouldn't try eating too much at any one time and that (b) everyone's appetite is different.

How many transformation and change programmes have you got going on right now?

Are you taking on too much at any one time?

Could you slow down and, in doing so, end up going faster and achieving more?

Are there any that you should just stop?

Don't get stuffed.

JOHN SPEDAN LEWIS

WAS A PUNK!

In the 1920s, (John) Spedan Lewis came to the conclusion that there needed to be a different model of capitalism, one that was fairer for all.

He decided that the John Lewis Partnership, which didn't include Waitrose at that time, should be put in trust for the benefit of all of the people that worked there.

Spedan Lewis' view of the world was that:

"If you put your people first, your people stay longer and are more committed, they're more loyal and because of that your customers get better service. That, in turn, helps deliver a profitable and sustainable business."

Both John Lewis and Waitrose, which is owned by the same trust, follow the same approach. Both have consistently been at the top, or near the top, of the most loved brands, and the most highly rated brands for customer satisfaction, for more than 10 years.

Now, achieving the same heights as these brands may not require putting your business in trust for the benefit of all of the people that worked there.

But, it may require something similarly radical if you want to achieve that.

What are you willing to do?

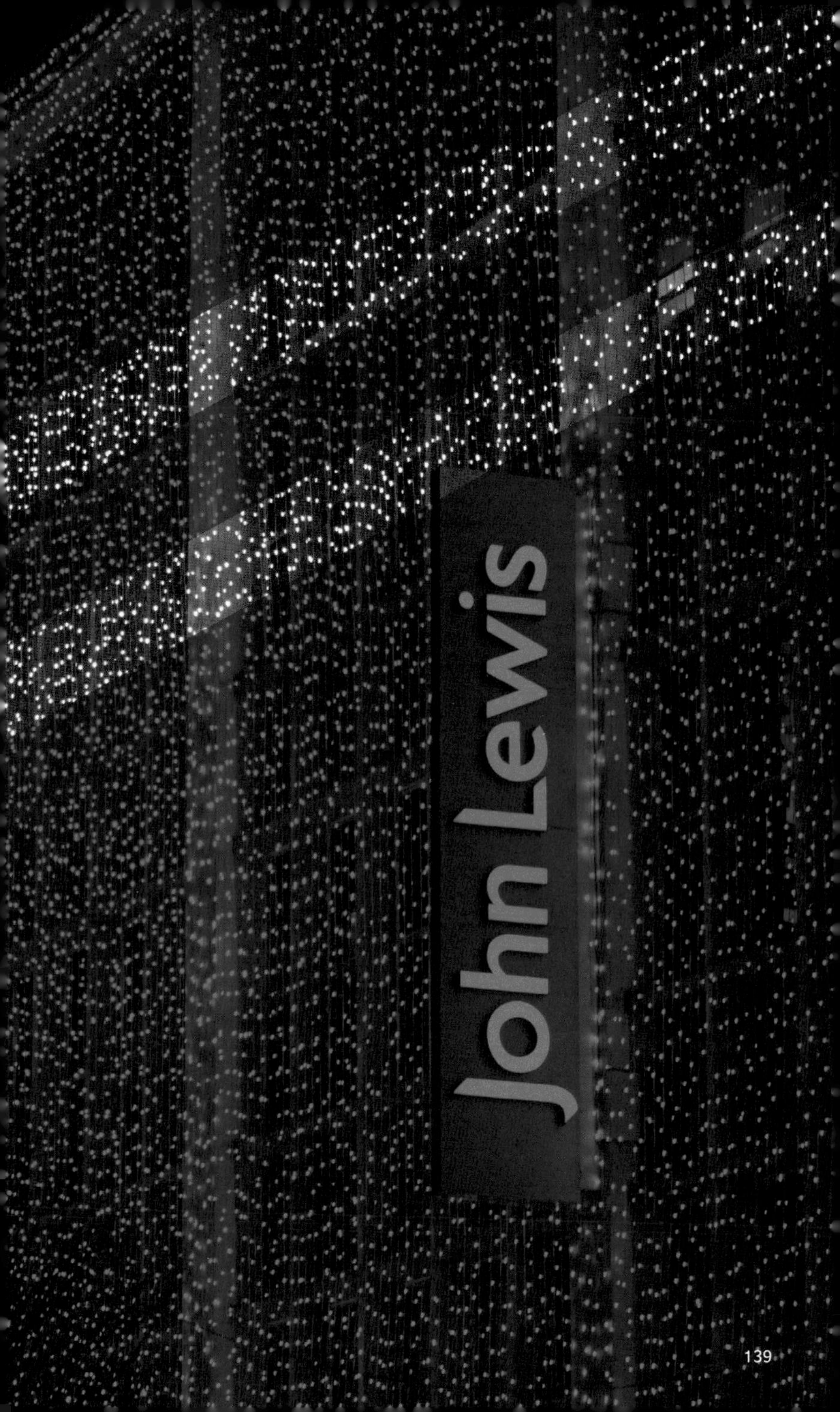
John Lewis

WOULD YOU LIKE
TO GO FOR LUNCH?

Siloed working is a common complaint in many organisations, and is often cited as being one of the main barriers to being able to deliver a consistent customer experience.

To overcome these sorts of barriers many firms opt for software solutions to promote better communication and increased collaboration across silos.

Many of these solutions are great.

But, what they don't tackle is the human relationship element that sits at the heart of most great teams and well-functioning organisations.

In his new book The Excellence Dividend, Tom Peters offers an ingenious and alternative way to solve siloed working.

Lunch.

He advocates that everyone in every organisation should spend as many of their lunchtimes as possible getting to know their other colleagues.

Think about it.

Imagine if you spent 50% of your lunches having a sandwich or a salad with a colleague that you didn't know.

Imagine the number of new connections you would establish.

Imagine the things you would learn and the number of new ways that you would establish to getting things done.

It's a simple but powerful idea, and one that will cost you no more than the price of a salad or a sandwich a couple of times a week.

What's not to like?

Who are you going to invite to lunch first?

Who will be second?

How are you going to encourage your colleagues to follow your lead?

DIY

This book does not claim to be
complete and have all of the answers.

We would like to start a 'movement'
of punks in the CX space.

So, make up your own 'track', share
it with us, join the movement and we
might even include your track in the
next volume ;)

Go on, give it a go and send your ideas to:
punkcxideas@adrianswinscoe.com

HONORARY CX PUNKS

Richard Wolfstrome

Oisin Lunny

Helen Le Voi

Jim Dawton

Richie Manu

Dr Simon Moore

Minter Dial

Stan Phelps

Neil Davey

Nikki Gatenby

Alex Genov

Dr Nicola Millard

Craig Hanna

James Lawther

Shaun Belding

Sheldon Yellen

John Spedan Lewis

Lord Mark Price

Rory Sutherland

Richard Shotton

Tom Peters

Paul Arden

Seth Godin

Dave Trott

Matt Prowse

....

[Insert your name here if you think you deserve it]

HONORARY CX PUNK COMPANIES

An incomplete list of companies that have a punk mindset:

Nike

Lush

John Lewis & Partners/Waitrose & Partners

Lidl in the UK

Timpsons in the UK

Zappos

first direct

citizen M

Wayfair

Simply Business

Voxpro

Zendesk

Buurtzorg

Semco

Patagonia

IAG

Gravity Payments

Tower Paddle Boards

Coventry Building Society

....

[Insert your company name here if you think you deserve it]

ABOUT ME

I'm a best-selling author, Forbes contributor and aspirant CX Punk. I've been growing and helping develop customer-focused large and small businesses for over 25 years now. I've previously worked for Shell, the FT and The Economist Group and have advised numerous large and small businesses around the world on how to improve their service and customer experience.

My clients have included TUI, the UK Government's Crown Commercial Service, NowTV, ITV, Pega, 1800Contacts, Talk Talk, Gazprom Energy, CIMA, Cancer Research, Bibby Financial Services, Harper Collins, Pearson, Consumers International and Costa Coffee amongst others.

I'm a frequent writer, interviewer, podcaster, conference speaker, panellist, chair and workshop leader on all things related to customer experience.

Previous books:

Rare Business: How Building Better Relationships with Your People and Your Customers Can Deliver Sustainable Growth - Published by RARE Publications in 2010 there are still a few copies lying around. Get in touch if you want to get hold of one. I particularly like the cartoons in the book which were done by the wife of an ex-student of mine.....that's a longish story for another time.

How to Wow: 68 Effortless Ways to Make Every Customer Experience Amazing - Published by Pearson in 2016 this is the best-selling one and the one that is responsible for my Mum and Dad now thinking that I have a proper job :)

You can find out more about me and get in touch at:

www.adrianswinscoe.com
www.punkcx.com
www.forbes.com/sites/adrianswinscoe/
uk.linkedin.com/in/adrianswinscoe
twitter.com/adrianswinscoe

Made in the USA
Coppell, TX
30 January 2020

15181017R00093